LOOK BEFORE YOU LEAP:
A Simple Dating Guide for A Healthy Relationship

REGINA STAFFORD, BCC

Copyright © 2013 by Regina Stafford, BCC

Look Before You Leap: A Simple Dating Guide for A Healthy Relationship
by Regina Stafford, BCC

Printed in the United States of America

ISBN 9781628713824

All rights reserved solely by the author. The author guarantees all contents are original and do not infringe upon the legal rights of any other person or work. No part of this book may be reproduced in any form without the permission of the author. The views expressed in this book are not necessarily those of the publisher.

Unless otherwise indicated, Bible quotations are taken from the New American Standard Bible (NASB). Copyright © 1999 by Zondervan Publisher.

www.xulonpress.com

TABLE OF CONTENTS

Endorsements v
A Few Thank You's ix
Look Before You Leap 11
Four Phases Of Dating 15
Phase 1 – Agape Love 19
Phase 2 – Philio Love 25
Phase 3 – Storge Love 29
Phase 4 – Eros Love (Final) 35
Notes 39
About The Author 43
Contact Information 45

ENDORSEMENTS

Regina Stafford has written a practical book on dating that is based on her experience with her husband Thomas, as well as much time spent counseling couples in our local church. She has seen firsthand the heartbreak and devastation that takes place when people mimic the world instead of the bible as their guide for healthy relationships. I especially pray that young people would embrace these principles!
~ Dr. Joseph G. Mattera, Presiding Bishop for Christ Covenant Coalition and Overseeing Bishop of Resurrection Church, Brooklyn, NY

I have known Regina Stafford for 10 years and find in her a generous heart full of grace and beauty and a hunger to see God's People living like God's People. Her extensive experience with marriage coaching and ministry with youth has developed a uniquely insightful perspective that she is sharing with us in *Look Before You Leap*. There is a lot of confusion among teens and

young adults today. Our culture is pulling them into a negative view of marriage and commitment and into a careless approach to sexuality. This booklet will be very useful for teens and young adults, parents and youth leaders. This is a topic that needs to be introduced to middle school age children before they embrace current sexual and relationship mores. This booklet is written in a manner that it can be used to address sensitive topics with biblical authority. I am looking forward to more thought provoking and practical guides from Regina.
~ Paul H. VanValin, PhD, Licensed Clinical Psychologist, President, Eden Counseling and Consultation and Eden Family Institute

Regina Stafford approaches this topic with many years' experience helping others develop successful relationships. The wisdom she shares has proven time and again to empower couples in their pursuit for healing, purpose and sustainability. Because the concepts are, at the same time, both practical and life changing, *Look Before You Leap* should be required reading for all singles, especially those considering marriage at any point in their lives. Engaged and pre-engaged couples on the journey to the altar and married couples struggling to find a "breath of fresh air" in their relationships will also benefit from understanding

the timeless insight Regina presents in a conversational and enjoyable format. Counselors, life coaches and clergy will all find this a useful resource in their toolboxes and I am excited about sharing it with our network of churches and non-profit agencies.
~ James C. Esposito, Founder and Executive Director New York Christian Resource Center

It has been said "things don't GO wrong, they START wrong" and I think truer words could not describe the problem ailing most relationships. Most relationships are built on foundations that are not sustainable, largely because the foundation consists primarily of erotic or romantic love to the exclusion of friendship and selfless love. As a certified life-coach and marriage counselor for over 20 years, Regina Stafford has seen the good, the bad and the ugly of relationships and in this book she offers sound advice to those seeking a better way forward. As you read this work, your understanding will be challenged and changed and so will your present and future relationship.
~ Kristian Hernandez, Pastor, Hope Church NYC

A FEW THANK YOU'S...

I want to thank My Lord Jesus for finding me, loving me and changing me. I love His Word that is filled with principles for every area of life which is the solid foundation I've built mine upon. He has proven His faithfulness time and time again; always there for me and always leaving me in awe.

I want to thank my husband Thomas who saw more in me than I saw in myself and always encouraged me to fly high and soar. I am humbled by how you love me and so grateful to God for our relationship and all He has taught us. I love you and what we share, and I love teaching others the principles we live by.

I want to thank my children, Thomas and Katie. I love you both so much. I love spending time with you guys; you not only make me laugh, but you challenge me to grow. You've been hearing about dating and marriage since you were kids and I pray your choice for your marriage partner is your very best friend.

To a few very special friends that made this book possible through their love, help, encouragement, input and prayers. You all hold a dear place in my heart and I am grateful you have been put in my life. Thank you Annie Burgos, James Esposito, Kristian Hernandez and Daisy Pedroza. You guys are the greatest cheerleaders!

A special thank you to Dianne Galasso for all of your hard work on this book. Your editing, re-editing and "eagle eye" have been invaluable to me. You were my answer to prayer to bring this project to life and in the process became a special friend too. (Where's the lampshade, lol).

LOOK BEFORE YOU LEAP
A Simple Dating Guide to a Healthy Relationship

When I first became a Christian many years ago, I wanted to do everything God's way. I wanted Him in the center of my life! As I began to study His word and grow in the Lord, it was clear to me that God has a blueprint for all areas of our lives, including our relationships. The Bible is full of guidance and wisdom for all relationships: marriages, parent/child, friendships, employer/employee and even business relationships. God lays out the path to follow for the greatest success in each of these areas offering principals to stand on, and trust in, through the good times and the rough patches. These principals and practical steps will keep you sure and steady (if you allow) as you put one foot in front of the other in your path of life.

While all these relationships are important in our lives, let's talk dating and courtship!

First, let's define these two terms. Dating and courtship are two different things.

Dating is a form of courtship that consists of social activities done by two people with the aim of assessing the other's suitability as a partner in life—for marriage. It basically refers to meeting and engaging in some mutually agreed upon social activity to get to know each other better!

Courtship is bringing dating to the next level! This is the period in time where the couple has dated and is now ready to develop and grow the relationship with the intent of marriage; seeking love with the *intent* to marry! Our culture has changed so dramatically over the years, along with the terminology for dating and courtship. Sometimes I laugh with my children (ages 21 and 14) at the different meanings of "hooking up"! This could actually be the reason why so many people on social networking sites list their relationship status as "complicated". It's complicated when you can't define it in the first place!

As overseers of The Family Ministry for over 25 years at our church, my husband and I have the opportunity to counsel and coach many couples pre- and post-marriage. We've met many couples who didn't utilize the dating/courting process as outlined by God, which often led to relational issues that brought them to our doorstep.

I've called the dating/courtship a process because I believe there is a clear step-by-step biblical process that starts at dating and either leads to the altar of marriage or the road of parting ways. When we meet with couples who are facing challenges in their relationship, one of the first questions we ask is what their dating and courtship season was like. Most of the time, the issues that brought them to counseling have been there all along, but the couples either chose not to look at them or they moved ahead so quickly that they didn't see them. You'd be surprised how many times we've heard "we thought it would get better once we got married" - NEVER ever believe this lie. Whatever issues are there before you say "I DO" will only intensify afterwards.

For the record, let me say that I don't believe in dating as a recreational sport. If you're just looking to have some fun with friends, then keep it in the friend zone. People get hurt when handled by someone who doesn't have an honest interest in them – get a hobby instead. When you feel like you're ready to share in another person's life, and are mature enough to know it's not just all about you any longer, then you're ready to

Look Before You Leap

---

date. With that said, it's my hope that this practical guide will help you move forward confidently, thoughtfully and prayerfully in your choice of a lifetime partner.

Our society today is very casual about dating and unfortunately, that casual attitude has given way to dating being all about one person, "you": your fun, your enjoyment, your feelings. If you're not having a good time (fun, fun, fun) then it's on to the next person. Now, I'm not saying not to have fun or that dating is not fun, but there is more. You have to care about another person's feelings, even if after getting to know them better you find you no longer want to move forward. Often, television portrays young adults running around being irresponsible and cruel, giving the perception that it's ok for that sort of behavior, but it isn't.

So, let's talk dating.

I've heard over and over couples say after a few dates they decide…"we're taking it slow". What does that mean? What does "slow" look like??

FOUR PHASES OF DATING

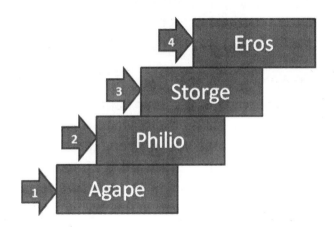

There are four types of love listed in the bible that I believe can be used as a guideline to not only lead you through the dating/courtship process, but to help you know rather quickly if you are entering into something that is good for you or that's not good for you, and thereby minimizing the pain and drama that can come with being in a relationship.

The four types of love in the bible are taken from the Greek language: *agape, philio, storge* and *eros*. Each type of love is a phase within the dating / courtship process and has specific purpose. We are going to look at each type of love (phase) to map out how to proceed (or not) to the next level in relationships. These phases will help you gauge if it's time to go to the next level, give the relationship more time in one phase or respectfully part ways.

Hosea 4:6 says that God's people perish for lack of knowledge. It's important to keep your head involved because choices made based solely on feelings can lead you in wrong directions. As the relationship moves forward, it's important to take stock from time to time to make sure you still want it to go in the direction it is going. God has given each of us a sound mind and judgment (1 Timothy 5:6) and He expects us to use It; following truth and good judgment will never lead you wrong. We are advised in Proverbs 4:23 to guard our hearts above all things; using good judgment and discernment is one way to do just that. I believe "LOOK BEFORE YOU LEAP" will help keep your heart protected until the right time so you can enjoy the journey without anxious thoughts and concerns. That's freedom!

Throughout all of these phases—*through this entire process*—from the initial thought of the possibility of dating a specific person—you should be praying, sometimes fasting and be accountable to someone who you have relationship with (trusted leader or Godly friend) who will keep you accountable for your actions as you move along this journey. Proverbs 11:14 says there is wisdom (and safety) in a multitude of counselors...it's very true.

PHASE 1 – AGAPE LOVE

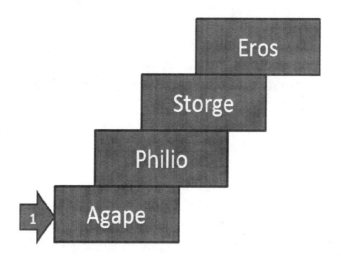

The first kind of love is called *agape* love. Agape love is the God kind of love often referring to general affection. This type of love is very general, kind and friendly towards one another. With agape love, you seek to be a blessing without self-benefit. God loves us this way and we are called to love others the same way — even strangers! It's unconditional and unhindered.

What does this look like?

Let's say, as you are being friendly and kind to those around you, there happens to be a particular person you begin to feel attracted to. That attraction starts with agape love and a general attention. It's a time of observation and recognition of one another. You watch from a bit of a distance to evaluate and discern if you should step closer or close the door.

How does this play out in practical terms?

For younger adults (late teens and 20's), a group of friends get together maybe at a church functions, at school or just out with a group of people on some outings. For this age group, you do a lot of things within a group setting with no pairing off alone. This is a great opportunity to observe the person you are attracted to and grow in friendship in a safe environment. It's important to be a good friend and learn how to keep a friend. If you're a 30+adult, this is where your judgment really comes in. Like the younger adults, it's also a time to observe the person you're attracted to, but older adults tend to spend more time one on one.

For all ages, this is the time to notice your potential partner's walk with the Lord. It's a great opportunity to really see his/her heart for God (is it genuine, do they want to serve Him, are they striving to learn and grow in the things of God). This is also the time to get to know them more personally with some questions like:

~ Do they go to school or work?

~ What are their life's goals?

~ Are they respectful?

~ Can they relate well to others?

~ Do they know how to give honor and to be accountable to someone?

Now, don't misunderstand, I'm not saying they have to be perfect in everything, but these are some very important qualities and characteristics that you'd want to see in someone before considering going to the next phase of a relationship. If they don't have real interest in the things of God, can't hold down a job, have no goals or vision for their life, is disrespectful, is rebellious to authority and rules and/or is easily angered, this is not someone you'd want to spend the rest of your life with – no matter how good looking they may be. It's time to shut the door!

At this point, no one gets hurt because you've taken the time to find out before getting more involved. Thank God for allowing you to see truth and saving you from a potential mess. The agape love phase is like looking before you leap; it's about keeping your eyes open and not falling in love or falling "head over heels" before it's time. This phase is wisely guarding your heart (when the heart leads, you become blind to everything else). Healthy relationships take two mature people who want to keep on maturing and growing in all areas of their lives and they BOTH (not just one) are submitted to God.

For the 30+ adults, doing things in groups is nice, but like I said earlier, they're more likely to have more one on one time. You can still guard your heart by doing casual things together. For instance, coffee houses, restaurants, shopping, Sporting events, etc., being in places where there are other people around. This reduces the potential to get into a situation that would be hard to get out of! So, stay out of each other's apartments; this is not the time to show off your "cooking skills" unless it's a dinner party for more than just the two of you. Human nature and feelings can make good judgment go right out the door if given the chance.

What happens when you've spent time together, enjoy each other and want to take things to the next level?

PHASE 2 – PHILIO LOVE

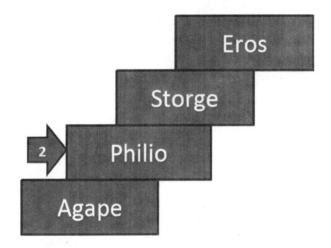

$\mathcal{T}$he second type of love is called philio love. This is a friendship love; a true meaningful friendship with give and take qualities. The desire to see each other more often grows. During this phase, you choose smaller settings where you can talk and get to know each other more intimately. This is the time to become more intimate in friendship with this person you are attracted to. Still no pairing off yet for the younger group and no house visits for those 30+-ers! Putting yourself in compromising situations only make it harder and more tempting for yourselves to get cozier than is good for a relationship at this point.

This is also a time to continue to watch their walk with the Lord and their relationships with others. You should also be getting a closer look at their work ethic and emotional maturity.

~ How well do they communicate and handle conflict?

~ How do they react or respond to what you deem as important in a relationship?

~ How do they treat you?

~ Are they still who you think they are or have they changed?

~ Do they have the same or similar values as you?

Hopefully you have a good sense of self-worth and accept nothing less than being treated extremely well. Through this phase, be honest with yourself and the person to whom you've become accountable to with the details of this relationship. This process needs to take time.

The bible says in Isaiah 28:16, that he who believes does not make hast. Whirlwind relationships will hold many unwanted surprises down the road; quite possibly some things you didn't sign up for, nor are equipped to handle.

How long before the next step? The answer is simple – as long as it needs to take for you to be sure that this is the direction you want to be going with this person. Despite the "feelings", a healthy dating relationship could take at least a year. Remember, we have been given a spirit of self-control and judgment (Galatians 5:22). I base this next statement on years of experience with couples who took the proper steps and those who didn't. Watching and waiting will help you gather all the information you need to make a well thought out decision.

During this phase, continue to keep your relationship in prayer and be open with your accountability partner. If you decide not to continue with this friendship, then have a conversation with the other person and part ways. At this point, there are still no deep rooted emotions and/or entanglements because you weren't officially "courting" yet. You can still remain friends without anyone getting hurt. If the relationship is going well and you like what you see, it's time to have the conversation and commit to courting each other exclusively.

PHASE 3 – STORGE LOVE

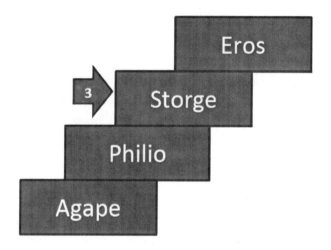

This love is called storge (pronounced store-gay) love. It's a familiar type of love with a deep and abiding affection; akin to feeling close like family. You speak on the phone more, spend more time with each other and go out alone much more often. Your conversations become much more heart felt where you share life experiences with one another. Talking about one's past is a great way to see what formed that person and how they became who they are today.

Side note: Spending more time alone at this point, again, requires wisdom on where you go what you do. This type of love and intimacy compliments phase 4 (eros love – the physical aspect of marriage), so don't put yourselves in tempting situations if you intend to wait until marriage before having a sexual relationship. Don't give the devil a place if you want to continue to move forward God's way as instructed in Ephesians 4:27. We've seen many well-meaning Christians fall into sexual sin at this point. It's a vulnerable and intimate time between a couple – so be wise!

This phase is where you have him/her home with your family for a holiday or just to spend family time together. You get to know each other's families better and get more involved with their lives. You will now get to see how they act in their own familiar surroundings.

~ How do they act towards their parents and siblings?

~ How do they act when their "hair is let down" or their "shoes are kicked off"?

~ How is their home?

~ Is he a momma's boy or is she a daddy's girl (do they act like mature adults around their family)?

~ Is he/she controlling, are they demanding of their own ways?

The old saying that says "I'm marrying the person and not their family" is a fallacy. Who and what you are, and who and what they are all come into a marital relationship whether you want it to or not. These are the people and situations that helped form that person and you'll have to deal with that for many years to come. If he/she has children from a previous relationship, what is the dynamic there? Although it's true that we are a product of our past, it's also true that we don't have to let it define our future. If the family has some bad patterns, but the individual you are dating shows you he/she is different (notice I said "shows" and not "says"), then you can talk about those things that you like and don't like and whether or not you want them in your relationship as you move forward. This is also important because you will learn if this person is willing to work on what's important to you. A great marriage takes teamwork. Are they a team player or do they think they're the MVP???

Life is a series of negotiations, choices, compromises, disappointments and failures. Having a partner who is willing to do whatever it takes to keep that relationship alive and healthy will make all the difference in a lasting and fulfilling marriage relationship.

Many important conversations need to happen in this phase.

~ Is there room for both of you to grow and excel?

~ Do you want children? How many? How soon?

~ Vision for the future, e.g., can the wife stay home with the children if she chooses? Are you both in agreement?

~ Where should we live...etc, etc, etc

Amos 3:3 asks how two can walk together unless they are in agreement. The more you communicate with each other and come into agreement on life's decisions, the better off you will be in

Phase 3 – Storge Love

the future. Marriage is actually a series of agreements which is where the foundation of running the home and family takes place. ONENESS! The bible also teaches that where there is unity, the Lord commands the blessings (Psalm 133:1-3 Paraphrased). Keep talking to each other, keep dreaming and sharing your hearts. If something isn't right, listen. Even though there may be some pain, it's still not too late to exit at this point if you need to; even though you've become close to one another, at this point, it's still better to depart now than after years of building a marriage and a home along with innocent children that might be in the picture. The pain from a divorce and a broken home is heartbreaking for all those involved.

Does the courtship process sound like hard work? It is, but considering that marriage can either be like heaven on earth or hell on earth, it's absolutely worth the effort. Even though it's a lot of work, it's still a process that should be enjoyed. Let it flow and grow, keeping your eyes open. If you put the work in now, you will reap a strong, solid relationship for years to come.

These are guidelines to keep you pointed in the right direction, not to lock you into a robotic checklist. Some people are willing to do more research in buying a car then they are in finding a life partner. If you truly want to do it God's way before you make a commitment that is meant to last a lifetime, then I want to encourage you to do the work. Commit to the process with your eyes wide open – both in the natural and the spirit.

When both of you are ready to take the next step.....

PHASE 4 – EROS LOVE (FINAL)

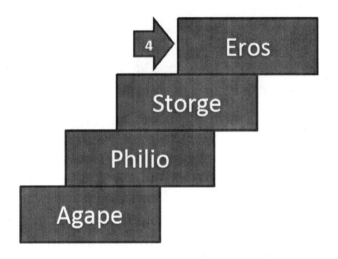

If things just keep getting better and better and you love what you are seeing, hearing and experiencing between the two of you, and you're connecting on so many levels concerning your futures, then you may be ready for the next step – MARRIAGE!

I cannot say this enough because it is so important: YOU MUST stay submitted to God in prayer and your accountability relationship. It is for your benefit not to be a loner when it comes to the most important relationship you will ever have, next to your relationship with God because sometimes others can see what we can be blinded to.

The final stage in the courtship relationship is *eros* or erotic love. This is the love saved for, and shared in, marriage according to the Word of God. It is the culmination or joining of two mature people ready to embark on their own journey together. People who enter eros love without the other loves in place may not ever get to the first 3 phases. It's always harder to work backwards once a physical relationship takes place to get those key elements for a healthy relationship. When there is a spiritual intimacy (agape love), a friendship intimacy (storge love) and a familiarly intimacy (philio love) that occurs, then the physical intimacy (eros love) in your marriage will be the highest enjoyment imaginable; an intimacy on all levels. It will be, as I heard one minister say, 3D sex (as opposed to a one dimensional sexual union, i.e., just the physical level)

Sadly, I have heard from too many divorced couples that they are "now" best friends with their ex-spouses; too bad the physical piece was the foundation instead of the final brick.

These guidelines are not a popular teaching in mainstream society today, in fact, they may even be hard to find in the church since so many churches hold different views on dating. It is my hope that this book will help us to better understand and adopt a healthy dating/courtship mentality which we can pass on, so that it will be a less confusing and complicated process. Biblical dating and courtship, I believe, is meant to be enjoyable and done responsibly. Granted, sometimes despite all your best efforts, "stuff" happens, but at least we can give our future marriages and families the best possible starting point, as well as a better understanding of why it's important to wait and it's not just being "old fashioned".

NOTES

I'd like to suggest making a Pros and Cons list. It may sound crazy, but there is a specific reason it can be helpful. Remember I said no one can change a person and that some things actually seem to intensify after you get married, well if you really want to "Look Before You Leap", then this is a helpful tool! After your list is made, take a look on the "CON" side and ask yourself this question "could I live with this person if he/she never changed from how they are right now?" – till death do us part!! This exercise could be a real eye opener.

PROS	CONS

ABOUT THE AUTHOR

Regina Stafford is a Life and Wellness Coach certified by New York University and Light University; Board Certified by The Center for Education and Credentialing. She is the Founder of Rewards Coaching, and on the Advisory Board of Children of the City, a community based advocacy organization helping underprivileged children in the Southern Brooklyn area.

Currently, Regina is a Manager and Counselor at a weight loss center helping individuals reach their health and wellness goals. She is also a leader in her local church and oversees The Family Ministry with her husband Thomas helping couples and families build a healthy, solid foundation.

Regina has worked with a very diverse population from entrepreneurs and professionals to those in the arts and entertainment industry. She has helped bring clarity to their many ideas and dreams, as well as offer practical steps to bring those dreams to life. Having a great understanding of the dynamics of relationships, Regina also works privately with couples and families who are seeking more healthy and rewarding interactions.

Regina lives in Brooklyn and has been married for 29 years to her husband, Thomas. They have two children, Thomas II and Katie. Her passion is to help people find their voice, identity and personal power enabling them to grow, dream and reach beyond where they are today.

CONTACT INFORMATION

Regina Stafford, BCC
Email: rs.coaching@aol.com

WEBSITE: www.rewardscoaching.com
FACEBOOK: Reward Coaching
TWITTER: ReginaS@rewardscoaching

Also Available:

MARRIAGE BUILDERS PROGRAM: A marriage training group for engaged and married couples. This is a six-week training group where we teach biblical principles for marriage.

LEADERS TRAINING: Training for Pastors, Elders and Leadership Teams. This is a seven-week course that teaches the basic principles of coaching for more authentic and effective Christian Leadership.

Please feel free to contact me with any questions, comments or for speaking engagements.

CPSIA information can be obtained at www.ICGtesting.com
Printed in the USA
BVOW02s0941030214

343653BV00006B/112/P